Business Succession Planning Guide

A Step by Step Checklist

By Meir Liraz

(Including 10 Special Bonuses)

Published by Liraz Publishing

www.BizMove.com

Copyright © Liraz Publishing. All rights reserved.

ISBN: 9781695632103

Table of Contents

1. Elements of an Effective Plan — 5
2. Putting the Pieces Together — 6
3. Implementing a Plan to Pass the Business to the Next Generation — 10
4. Planning for the Sale of a Business — 12
5. Financial Considerations of a Succession Plan — 16

Supplements:

6. How to Make the Right Decisions — 21
7. Improving Your Delegation Skills — 27
Appendix: Special free Bonuses — 32

MEIR LIRAZ

1. Elements of an Effective Plan

Criteria

What do you want to accomplish?

Is your small business a "hobby" or a "business?"

Time Frame

When to start your plan.

Knowing where you are in the small business life cycle.

Players

Who is involved in the decision making?

Who will be affected?

"People support what they help create."

Evaluation

When will you know that you've made it?

Without a plan, you won't know where you're going or how to get there.

2. Putting the Pieces Together

Define Owner/Founder Goals and Business Goals

What do I want as my business grows?

Do I have a vision of the future?

Have I communicated the vision to others?

Analyze Your Business

Structure

Market

Operation Policies

Personnel

Financial Condition

Create an "Advisory Team" to Help Create/Sell/Implement the Plan

"Two Heads are Better than One -- Three Heads Improve the Vision."

Staff for Strength -- Marketing, Legal, Financial, Insurance.

Develop a Time Line with Key Steps

Keep focused on the ultimate goal -- the perpetuation of your business and personal financial security.

Determine If Owner/Founder Goals Differ from Business Goals

Does the business drive the owner or does the owner drive the business?

Analyze Owner/Founder's Personal Assets, Estate Plan, Life Mission

Do individual goals clash with family or business goals/needs?

Be Mindful of the Possible Outcomes of Your Plan

Who will be affected -- to what extent?

Family members.

Stakeholder(s).

Market.

Employees.

Competitors.

When/How will You Communicate Your Plan?

Information minimizes confusions, distrust, uneasiness.

Examine Your Plan from a Strategic View

Strengths.

Weaknesses.

Opportunities.

Threats.

Create Measures to Evaluate/Provide Feedback

Should be:

Concrete

Specific

Measurable

Create Development Program So Successor Doesn't Begin "Cold Turkey" Passing the Reins

Have a transition period.

Mentor the new leader (s)

Answer Some Questions

Who am I?

What am I?

Why do I exist?

3. Implementing a Plan to Pass the Business to the Next Generation

Determine Goals/Objectives

Do you want to give up control?

Can you continue to manage daily operations?

Determine What is Best for You and the Business

Is it time to "pass the baton?"

Are you and/or your business being hurt by remaining on?

Examine Goals/Objectives of Family Members

Will they continue to wait for "their time?"

Avoid the Pitfalls

Family tensions.

Lack of personal financial security.

Selecting an inappropriate successor.

Setting up the successor to fail.

What to do When It's Time to Move On

Solicit objective input from advisors, family, business associates.

Set up criteria for successor.

Communicate decision to all parties.

Create clear agreement with successor to address steps, tome lines, financial considerations.

Begin relinquishment of control.

Set up program to mentor, train, educate successor.

Implement the financial agreement with the successor.

Turn business over to successor.

Create vehicle to allow you to "keep in touch."

4. Planning for the Sale of a Business

What are the Owner's Personal Goals

Consider retirement/using the business to provide security for the family, etc.

Key issue: how does the business fit within those goals?

Will the owner be able to will/gift the business to the family?

Is owner dependent business income for costs of living?

Does owner have resources to live independent of the business?

In Most Situations the Owner is Dependent on the Business

Owner must continue to work or it must be sold (cashed out).

Determining Accurate Business Value is Key

Once value is determined, compare to owners goals/needs.

Supplemental steps may need to be taken.

Steps to Take for Any Sale Plan

Determine and groom an appropriate successor.

"Sell" the plan to the appropriate parties.

Determine appropriate sales method:

Cross purchase (agreement between owners);

Redemption (agreement between owners/business);

"Wait and see, buy-sell (Buy-sell is in place but method determined at a later date).

Execute binding buy-sell agreement that can handle all contingencies:

lifetime sale;

sale at death;

sale in case of disability.

If Business Value Cannot Support Goals, Consider Alternatives

Remaining with the business, drawing salary beyond normal retirement.

Issues in this situation:

Will owner pass operations management

over/continue to draw salary?

Will owner completely release control of business or interferes with daily operations?

Will management retain dollars for expansion/investment, while passive owner pulls cash from company?

What impact will this have on the business value?

Other Alternatives

Selling company/receive rental income from company land?

Reaching negotiated agreement/roles passive owner and management will play.

Selling the business through an installment sale.

Owner may draw during working years and invest to lessen dependence on the business value:

qualified plans;

non-qualified plans;

private pension plans (executive bonus);

split dollar arrangements;

non-qualified deferred compensation.

5. Financial Considerations of a Succession Plan

Succession Plan Must Address Financial and Tax Issues

Without a funded succession plan any approach can be tenuous.

Three Basic Approaches

Sale

Gift/Will

Liquidation

Liquidation is Least Advantageous

Business being dissolved, fewer dollars received than from the business as a going concern.

Dollars come from the value of tangible assets.

Nothing is received for the value of the ongoing enterprise.

Usually only taken where there is little likelihood of sale/no heirs to take over the business.

Wherever possible, owner should have alternative resources for retirement as the liquidation value may prove insufficient.

Potential Buyers of the Business

Co-owners.

Family members (who also might receive shares as gifts).

Third party/competitors.

Methods Used to Sell the Business

Cash.

One time payment or installments;

Generally, dollars come from the business or from buyer's assets or salary.

Borrowed funds.

effect same as cash to seller;

buyer must pay interest to a lender (as opposed to interest to the seller under an installment sale).

Sinking fund.

dollars set aside in investment account, allowed to grow.

avoids interest payments with borrowed funds or

installment sale.

asset growth taxable/may be insufficient in the event of a premature sale (due to death, disability, etc.).

Insurance.

premium payments can take the place of a sinking fund;

can be permanent or term insurance;

permanent insurance provides tax deferred cash value growth

cash value can be used for a down payment;

"self completing" in the event of a premature death;

disability income buyout can handle disability issues.

Buy Sell Agreements Take Two Basic Approaches

Cross Purchase

Redemption Choosing correct approach involves:

specific company/owner needs/goals;

income tax consequences;

gift/estate tax consequences;

alternative minimum tax.

Gifting/Willing a Business in Family Situations

Relative may need to buy out parent to ensure parent retirement funds.

When parents can afford to gift/will the business to their child they must consider several items:

the parent will often try to balance inheritance received by children not involved in the business;

are there sufficient assets to do so;

is there a need to "create" an estate to will to those children;

often done with insurance options.

Businesses often large illiquid assets/difficult to sell before estate taxes are due.

Insurance can handle estate taxes/allow less pressured sale.

Option to wait until death and will the business.

Raises issues related to retaining control (and management) if the older generation keeps control of the business interest.

Supplements:

6. How to Make the Right Decisions

Everyone is a decision maker. We all rely on information, and techniques or tools, to help us in our daily lives. When we go out to eat, the restaurant menu is the tool that provides us with the information needed to decide what to purchase and how much to spend. Operating a business also requires making decisions using information and techniques - how much inventory to maintain, what price to sell it at, what credit arrangements to offer, how many people to hire.

Decision making in business is the systematic process of identifying and solving problems, of asking questions and finding answers. Decisions usually are made under conditions of uncertainty. The future is not known and sometimes even the past is suspect. This guide opens the door for business owners and managers to learn about the variety of techniques which can be used to improve decision making in a world of uncertainty, change, and uncontrollable circumstances.

A General Approach to Decision Making

Whether a scientist, an executive of a major corporation, or a small business owner, the general approach to systematically solving problems is the same. The following 7 step approach to better management decision making can be used to study nearly all problems faced by a business.

1. State the problem

A problem first must exist and be recognized. What is the problem and why is it a problem. What is ideal and how do current operations vary from that ideal. Identify why the symptoms (what is going wrong) and the causes (why is it going wrong). Try to define all terms, concepts, variables, and relationships. Quantify the problem to the extent possible. If the problem, not accurately and quickly filling customer orders, try to determine how many orders were incorrectly filled and how long it took to fill them.

2. Define the Objectives

What are the objectives of the study. Which objectives are the most critical. Objectives usually are stated by an action verb like to reduce, to increase, or to improve. Returning to the customer order problem, the major objectives would be: 1) to increase the percentage of orders filled correctly, and 2) to reduce the time it takes to process and order. A subobjective could include to simplify and streamline the order filling process.

3. Develop a Diagnostic Framework

Next establish a diagnostic framework, that is, decide what methods are going to be used, what kinds of information are needed, and how and where the information is to be found. Is there going to be a customer survey, a review of company documents, time and motion tests, or something else. What are the assumptions (facts assumed to be correct) of the study. What are the criteria used to judge the study. What time, budget, or other constraints are there. What kind of quantitative or other specific techniques are going to be used to analyze the data. (Some of which will be covered shortly). In other words, the diagnostic framework establishes the scope and methods of the entire study.

4. Collect and Analyze the Data

The next step is to collect the data (by following the

methods established in Step 3. Raw data is then tabulated and organized to facilitate analysis. Tables, charts, graphs, indexes and matrices are some of the standard ways to organize raw data. Analysis is the critical prerequisite of sound business decision making. What does the data reveal. What facts, patterns, and trends can be seen in the data. Many of the quantitative techniques covered below can be used during the step to determine facts, patterns, and trends in data. Of course, computers are used extensively during this step.

5. Generate Alternative Solutions

After the analysis has been finished, some specific conclusions about the nature of the problem and its resolution should have been reached. The next step is to develop alternative solutions to the problem and rank them in order of their net benefits. But how are alternatives best generated. Again, there are several well established techniques such as the Nominal Group Method, the Delphi Method and Brainstorming, among others. In all these methods a group is involved, all of whom have reviewed the data and analysis. The approach is to have an informed group suggesting a variety of possible solutions.

6. Develop an Action Plan and Implement

Select the best solution to the problem but be certain to understand clearly why it is best, that is, how it achieves the objectives established in Step 2 better than its alternatives. Then develop an effective method (Action Plan) to implement the solution. At this point an important organizational consideration arises - who is going to be responsible for seeing the implementation through and what authority does he have. The selected manager should be responsible for seeing that all tasks, deadlines, and reports are performed, met, and written. Details are important in this step: schedules, reports, tasks, and communication are the key elements of any action plan. There are several techniques available to decision makers implementing an action plan. The PERT method is a way of laying out an entire period such as an action plan. PERT will be covered shortly.

7. Evaluate, obtain Feedback and Monitor

After the Action Plan has been implemented to solve a problem, management must evaluate its effectiveness. Evaluation standards must be determined, feedback channels developed, and monitoring performed. This Step should be done after 3 to 5 weeks and again at 6 months. The goal is to answer the bottom line question. Has the problem been solved?

7. Improving Your Delegation Skills

Derived from Latin, delegate means "to send from." When delegating you are sending the work "from" you "to" someone else. Effective delegation Skills will not only give you more time to work on your important opportunities, but you will also help others on your team learn new skills.

Here are some tips that will help you improve your delegation skills - delegation of work.

- Delegation helps people grow underneath you in an organization and thus pushes you even higher in management. It provides you with more time, and you will be able to take on higher priority projects.

- Delegate whole pieces or entire job pieces rather than simply tasks and activities.

- Clearly define what outcome is needed, then let individuals use some creative thinking of their own as to how to get to that outcome.

- Clearly define limits of authority that go with the delegated job. Can the person hire other people to work with them? Are there spending constraints?

- Clear standards of performance will help the person know when he or she is doing exactly what is expected.

- When on the receiving end of delegation, work to make your boss' job easier and to get the boss promoted. This will enhance your promotability also.

- Assess routine activities in which you are involved. Can any of them be eliminated or delegated?

- Never underestimate a person's potential. Delegate slightly more than you think the person is capable of handling. Expect them to succeed, and you will be pleasantly surprised more frequently than not.

- Expect completed staff work from the individuals reporting to you. That is, they will come to you giving you alternatives and suggestions when a problem exists rather than just saying "Boss, what should we do?"

- Do not avoid delegating something because you cannot give someone the entire project. Let the person start with a bite size piece, then after learning and doing that, they can accept larger pieces and larger areas of responsibility.

- Agree on a monitoring or measurement procedure that will keep you informed as to progress on this project because you are ultimately still responsible for it and need to know that it is progressing as it should. In other words-If you can't measure it don't delegate it.

- Keep your mind open to new ideas and ways of doing things. There just might be a better way than the way something has previously been done.

- Delegation is not giving an assignment. You are asking the person to accept responsibility for a project. They have the right to say no.

- Encourage your people to ask for parts of your job.

- Never take back a delegated item because you can do it better or faster. Help the other person learn to do it better.

- Agree on the frequency of feedback meetings or reports between yourself and the person to whom you are delegating. Good communication will assure ongoing success.

- Delegation strengthens your position. It shows you are doing your job as a manager-getting results with others. This makes you more promotable.

- Delegation is taking a risk that the other person might make a mistake, but people learn from mistakes and will be able to do it right the next time. Think back to a time a project was delegated to you and you messed it up. You also learned a valuable lesson.

- Find out what the talents and interests of your people are and you will be able to delegate more intelligently and effectively.

- A person will be more excited about doing a project when they came up with the idea of how to do it, than if the boss tells them how to do it.

- Be sensitive to upward delegation by your staff. When they ask you for a decision on their project, ask them to think about some alternatives which you will then discuss with them. This way responsibility for action stays with the staff member.

- Don't do an activity that someone else would be willing to do for you if you would just ask them.

- "Push" responsibility down in a caring helpful way.

- Remember, you are not the only one that can accomplish an end result. Trust others to be capable of achieving it.

- Break large jobs into manageable pieces and delegate pieces to those who can do them more readily.

- Keep following up and following through until the entire project is done. Break large jobs into manageable pieces and delegate pieces to those who can do them more readily.

- Resist the urge to solve someone else's problem. They need to learn for themselves. Give them suggestions and perhaps limits but let them take their own action.

Appendix: Special Free Bonuses

You can access your free bonuses here:

https://www.bizmove.com/bizgifts.htm

Here's what you get:

#1 How to Be a Good Manager and Leader; 120 Tips to improve your Leadership Skills (Leadership Video Guide).

Learn how to improve your leadership skills and become a better manager and leader. Here's how to be the boss people want to give 200 percent for. In this video you'll discover 120 powerful tips and strategies to motivate and inspire your people to bring out the best in them.

#2 Small Business Management: Essential Ingredients for Success (eBook Guide)

Discover scores of business management tricks, secrets and shortcuts. This Ebook guide does far more than impart knowledge - it inspires action.

#3 How to Manage Yourself for Success; 90 Tips to Better Manage Yourself and Your Time (Self Management Video Guide)

You are responsible for everything that happens in your life. Learn to accept total responsibility for yourself. If you don't manage yourself, then you are letting others have control of your life. In this video you'll discover 90 powerful tips and strategies to better manage yourself for success.

#4 80 Best Inspirational Quotes for Success (Motivational Video Guide)

For this video we scanned thousands of motivational and inspirational quotes to bring you this collection of the best 80 motivational quotes for success in life.

#5 Top 10 Habits to Adopt From Highly Successful People (Self Growth Video Guide)

In this video you'll discover the top 10 habits of highly successful people that you can adopt and achieve success in your life.

#6 Personal Branding: How to Make a Killer First Impression (Self Promotion Video Guide)

This video deals with personal branding. While promoting your personal brand, you'll discover in this video the ten most effective things you can do to make the best first impression possible.

#7 How to Advance Your Career 10 Times Faster (Career Advancement Video Guide)

The most important thing to remember about your

career today is that you need to be responsible for your own future. In this video you'll discover 10 powerful strategies to advance your career faster.

#8 How to Get Success in Life; 10 Strategies to Attract the Life You Want (Self Actualization Video Guide)

To have more, we must be more of who we are. The secret is in the doing; none of it matters until we do something about it. In this video you'll discover 10 powerful strategies to attract the life you want.

#9 A Comprehensive Package of Business Tools

Here's a collection featuring dozens of business related templates, worksheets, forms, and plans; covering finance, starting a business, marketing, business planning, sales, and general management.

#10 People Management Skills: How to Deal with Difficult Employees (Managing People Video Guide)

Problem behavior on the part of employees can erupt for a variety of reasons. In this video you'll discover the top ten ideas for dealing with difficult employees.